Coping *with* Loneliness *workbook*

Facilitator Reproducible Guided Self-Exploration Activities

Ester R. A. Leutenberg
& John J. Liptak, Ed. D.

Whole Person Associates

101 West 2ⁿᵈ Street, Suite 203
Duluth MN 55802

800-247-6789

Books@WholePerson com
WholePerson com

Coping with Loneliness Workbook
Facilitator Reproducible Guided Self-Exploration Activities

Printed in the United States of America

Editorial Director: Carlene Sippola
Art Director: Joy Morgan Dey

Library of Congress Control Number: 2014954892
ISBN: 978-1-57025-322-5

Using This Book

Human beings are social by nature and need human interaction and connectedness. When people experience adequate levels of human interaction and connectedness, they feel a sense of satisfaction. On the other hand, when people are experiencing inadequate levels of interaction and connectedness, they feel lonely – something's missing.

Therefore, loneliness is a noticeable difference between people's desired level of social interaction and the actual level of social interaction. Loneliness is a sense of connection to others who help to satisfy one's needs. It is the feeling of no one to talk, relate or share with – even though people are all around. Being with loved ones does not guarantee absence of loneliness.

Loneliness is not synonymous with being alone. People who are alone are by themselves and not with other people. Some people view aloneness as a positive and others see it as negative. (See Part II, Chapter 4)

In our society filled with people who communicate primarily with a wide variety of technology, face-to-face social interaction has become less common, feelings of connectedness are rare, and people are lonelier than ever before. Technology can provide a false sense of being connected twenty-four hours a day, seven days a week. This feeling of virtual connection, however, may be deceiving, and people benefit with social face-to-face connections with other people.

Reasons People Experience Loneliness

People experience loneliness for many different reasons.

Most of these reasons are related to feeling a lack of social support and fall into five basic categories:

- **Life Changes** – Loneliness often occurs in the midst of major life changes such as loss of loved ones, moving to a new city, or not being able to work because of an illness or disability. These types of major life changes often encourage people to meet others.

- **Getting Older** – As people age, they experience the death of friends and family, often feel as if they have fewer people who share their life experiences.

- **Inadequate Social Skills** – When people are unable to communicate with others, because they have weak social skills, they are at risk for loneliness. A lack of adequate social skills can make it difficult for people to develop and maintain relationships with others.

- **Personality Characteristics** – People often are shy or lack the power of self-esteem to make friends easily, and therefore receive fewer responses and less support from other people.

- **Situational** – People often experience loneliness when they are surrounded by people who have different ideas, values and interests. Therefore, when people do not have friends, family members, and acquaintances with whom to share experiences, they perceive themselves to be different, and feel lonely.

Two Types of Loneliness

Almost everyone will experience loneliness from time to time. Different forms of loneliness exist.

Situational Loneliness –people feel lonely due to a situation or experience. This is a temporary situation. An example would be moving to a new city where a person does not have any friends and has not made any acquaintances. Even though this situation brings on feelings of loneliness, these feelings will naturally disappear once the person has made new friends. This state of loneliness is usually a transient form of loneliness that changes as the situation or circumstances change.

Chronic Loneliness – This is a form of loneliness that persists over time, regardless of the situation or circumstances. This chronic form of loneliness usually results from having a weak or non-existent support system, a lack of social skills, shyness, and/or low self-confidence. An example would be a person who lacks the self-confidence to initiate conversations when meeting new people, or a person who fears being alone. This type of loneliness often requires the person to take action and build a new set of social skills.

A specific type of this loneliness involves people with mental health issues. Even if they have a great support system and are surrounded by those who care, their issues cause them to feel alienated and lonely. They need to see a medical professional if it continues.

Symptoms of Lonely Feelings

As loneliness becomes a bigger problem for people on all levels of society, it is important to distinguish the specific symptoms of loneliness. Because loneliness is an extreme emotional state in which people experience powerful feelings of isolation from others, it is accompanied by a variety of thoughts and feelings. People who are lonely will exhibit many of the following symptoms:

- Crying a lot of the time
- Feeling "hollow" inside
- Feeling alienated from other people
- Feeling as if you are alone, even though you are surrounded with others
- Feeling as if you are not accepted
- Feeling as if you are not as worthwhile
- Feeling as if you are not loved.
- Feeling as if you cannot make friends or build stronger relationships with acquaintances
- Feeling as if you do not have the same interests and values as those around you
- Feeling as if you have nobody with whom to share personal concerns and experiences
- Feeling cutoff or disconnected
- Feeling damaged and unloved
- Feeling empty
- Feeling lost with no direction
- Feeling physical pain akin to a "broken heart"
- Feeling sad

Effects of Loneliness

Negative feelings of loneliness can lead to a variety of other health-related concerns and stress-related conditions including heart disease, high blood pressure and stroke. In addition, is often related to addiction, various forms of anti-social behavior, disrupted sleep patterns and various mental-health conditions. People experiencing long-term (chronic) form of loneliness are more susceptible to experiencing these wider effects of loneliness. If your participants are experiencing any of these effects, suggest they see a medical professional.

In order to deal successfully with all of the types of loneliness, people must find creative ways of coping. The *Coping with Loneliness Workbook* provides assessments and self-guided activities to help participants learn useful skills for coping creatively with the various types of loneliness. Many choices of self-exploration activities are provided for participants to determine which best suit their unique needs.

Format of Workbook

The *Coping with Loneliness Workbook* contains assessments and guided self-exploration activities for a variety of populations to help participants cope more effectively with the feelings and effects of loneliness.

Each chapter of this workbook begins with an annotated Table of Contents with notes and examples for the facilitator. Each chapter contains two primary elements:
1) a set of assessments to help participants gather information about themselves in a focused situation.
2) a set of guided self-exploration activities to help participants process information and learn ways of coping with loneliness.

Assessments

Each chapter begins with an assessment that provides participants with valuable information about themselves. These assessments help identify productive and unproductive patterns of behavior and life skills, and guide development of an awareness of ways to interact with the world. Assessments provide a path to self-discovery through participants' exploration of their unique traits and behaviors. The purpose of these assessments is not to categorize people, but to allow them to explore various elements that are critical for success in coping with loneliness in everyday life. This workbook contains self-assessments and not tests. Traditional tests measure knowledge and elicit either right or wrong responses. For the assessments provided in this book, remind participants that there are no right or wrong answers. These assessments ask only for opinions or attitudes about topics related to a variety of coping skills and abilities.

The assessments in this workbook are based on self-reported data. In other words, the accuracy and usefulness of the information is dependent on the information that participants provide honestly about themselves. All of the assessments in this workbook are designed to be administered, scored, and interpreted by the participants as a starting point for them to begin to learn more about themselves and their coping skills. Remind participants that the assessments are exploratory exercises and not a determination of abilities. These assessments are not a substitute for professional assistance. If you feel any of your participants need more assistance than you can provide, please refer them to an appropriate professional.

As your participants begin the assessments in this workbook give these instructions:

- There is no time limit for completing the assessments. You may work at your own pace. Allow yourself time to reflect on your results and how they compare to what you already know about yourself.
- Do not answer the assessments as you think others would like you to answer them or how you think others see you. These assessments are for you to reflect on your life and explore some of the barriers that are keeping you from living a less lonely life.
- Assessments are powerful tools, but only if you are honest with yourself. Take your time and be truthful in your responses so that your results are an actual reflection of you. Your level of commitment in completing the assessments honestly will determine how much you learn about yourself.
- Before completing each assessment, be sure to read the instructions. The assessments have similar formats, but they have different scales, responses, scoring instructions and methods for interpretation.
- Finally, remember that learning about yourself should be a positive and motivating experience. Don't stress about taking the assessments or about the discovery of your results. Just respond honestly and learn as much about yourself as you can.

(Continued on the next page)

Format of Workbook *(Continued)*

Guided Self-Exploration Activities

Guided self-exploration activities assist participants in self-reflection and enhance self-knowledge, identify ongoing and potential ineffective behaviors, and teach more effective ways of coping. Guided self-exploration is designed to help participants make a series of discoveries that lead to increased social and emotional competencies, as well as to serve as an energizing way to help participants grow personally and professionally. These brief, easy-to-use self-reflection tools are designed to promote insight and self-growth.

Many different types of guided self-exploration activities are provided for you to pick and choose the activities most needed by, and most appealing to, your participants.

The unique features of self-guided exploration activities make them usable and appropriate for a variety of individual sessions and group sessions.

Features of Guided Self-Exploration Activities

- **Quick, easy and rewarding to use** – These guided self-exploration activities are designed to be an efficient, appealing method for motivating participants to explore information about themselves - including their thoughts, feelings, and behaviors - in a relatively short period of time.

- **Reproducible** – Because the guided self-exploration activities can be reproduced by the facilitator, no more than the one book is needed. You may photocopy as many pages as you wish for your participants. If you want to add or delete words on a page, make one photocopy, white out and/or write your own words, and then make photocopies from your personalized master.

- **Participative** – These guided self-exploration activities help people to focus their attention quickly, aid them in the self-reflection process, and guide them in learning new and more effective ways of coping.

- **Motivating to complete** – The guided self-exploration activities are designed to be an energizing way for participants to engage in self-reflection and learn about themselves. Various activities and modalities are included to enhance the learning process related to developing important social and emotional competency skills.

- **Low risk** – The guided self-exploration activities are designed to be less threatening than formal assessments and structured exercises. They are user-friendly; participants will generally feel more aware and motivated after completing these activities.

- **Adaptable to a variety of populations** – The guided self-exploration activities can be used with many different populations and can be tailored to meet the needs of the specific population with whom you work.

- **Focused** – Each guided self-exploration activity is designed to focus on a single coping issue, thus enhancing the experience for participants.

- **Flexible** – The guided self-exploration activities are flexible and can be used independently or to supplement other types of interventions.

Chapter Elements

The *Coping with Loneliness Workbook* is designed to be used either independently or as part of an integrated curriculum. You may administer any of the assessments and the guided self-exploration activities to an individual or a group with whom you are working, or you may administer any of the activities over one or more days. Feel free to pick and choose those assessments and activities that best fit the outcomes you desire.

The first page of each chapter begins with a Table of Contents annotated with ideas and examples for the facilitator.

Assessments – Assessments with scoring directions and interpretation materials begin each chapter. The authors recommend that you begin presenting each topic by asking participants to complete the assessment. Facilitators can choose one or more, or all of the activities relevant to their participants' specific needs and concerns.

Guided Self-Exploration Activities – Practical questions and activities to prompt self-reflection and promote self-understanding are included after each of the assessments. These questions and activities foster introspection and promote pro-social behaviors and coping skills. The activities in this workbook are tied to the assessments so that you can identify and select activities quickly and easily.

The activities are divided into four chapters to help you identify and select assessments easily and quickly:

Chapter 1: Level of Loneliness

This chapter helps participants identify the extent of their loneliness and explore activities to cope with their loneliness.

Chapter 2: Personal Characteristics

This chapter helps participants identify their various personal characteristics that are tied to feelings of loneliness.

Chapter 3: Coping with Loneliness

This chapter helps participants identify the ways they can cope more effectively with loneliness in their lives.

Chapter 4: Alone Time

This chapter helps participants identify the differences between *loneliness* and *being alone*, and assists them to develop ways of enjoying their time, alone or with others. *My Alone-Time Positive Feelings*, page 82, and *My Alone-Time Negative Feelings*, page 83, can be used as pre- and post-tests, or used with each chapter.

Our thanks to these professionals who make us look good!

Reviewers: Carol Butler, MS Ed, RN, C, Rachel K. Kreger, MS, LPCC, Eric T. Wittenberg, MSW, LICSW

Editor and Lifelong Teacher: Eileen Regen

Art Director: Joy Dey

Editorial Director: Carlene Sippola

And special thanks to ...

Proofreader Extraordinaire: Jay Leutenberg and **Brain-Stormers:** The Atkin Family

Table of Contents

Level of Loneliness

Personal Characteristics

Table of Contents *(continued)*

Coping with Loneliness

Coping with Alone Time

Level of Loneliness

Example

Healthy Ways I Can Express Emotions	How I Could Begin Today	How I Could Further Engage in the Activity
Creative Activities	I enjoy taking photos of nature and animals.	I could join the photography club in my community. I also think I would like to go camping more, and take pictures of my trips.

Example

Unhealthy Activities	How Do You Think They Help You	What You Could Be Doing Instead
I drink alcohol	I feel less inhibited when I drink, and I am more likely to talk to other people.	I have several neighbors I have never met. I could bake something and take it to them and get to know them better.

Table of Contents and Facilitator Notes

Situations	Who Is Around?	Why Do I Feel Lonely in This Situation?
When I am at work	*Six co-workers in my office*	*I have never made an attempt to get to know them, and I have avoided being overly friendly. I will ask them to lunch!*

After the handout is completed, ask participants who are willing to share about the time when they felt the loneliest, and the major feelings associated with that time.

Prior to distributing the handout, ask the group members if they know the differences between loneliness and solitude. Write the various answers on the board.

After completing the handout, ask participants if they found it easy or difficult to describe their dissatisfaction with their family and friends, and why they found it easy or difficult.

Ask the group for a show of hands of those who journal. Ask those who do journal if they find it satisfying, and ask them to talk about it. If no one finds journaling satisfying, ask why. Talk about the benefits of journaling.

After completing the handouts, ask participants for volunteers willing to share what upcoming social event they are facing and how visualization can help them to overcome their fears.

After completing the handout, ask for a show of hands to indicate the types of technology participants are using most often and how the various technologies help them to feel connected or disconnected. Ask who would like to share their answers with the group.

Prior to distributing handout, ask participants to share their thoughts about the relationship between loneliness and feeling unloved.

Ask participants to stand in a circle and take each other's hands to form a circle. Now, ask them who they would like to include in their social circle and why.

Ask participants to think about pets they have had in the past and how these pets helped them to be less lonely. Ask willing participants to share their pet stories.

Level of Loneliness Scale
Introduction and Directions

Loneliness is the absence or perceived absence of satisfying social relationships, accompanied by stress and psychological distress because of this lack of relationships. People who are lonely experience powerful feelings of emptiness and isolation.

This assessment contains 22 statements that describe feelings associated with loneliness. Read each of the statements and decide whether or not the statement describes you. If the statement **does** describe you, circle the number under the TRUE column next to that item. If the statement **does not** describe you, circle the number under the FALSE column next to that item.

In the following example, the circled number under TRUE indicates the statement is descriptive of the person completing the inventory.

	TRUE	FALSE
I feel as if nobody likes me.	(1)	2

This is not a test. Since there are no right or wrong answers, do not spend too much time thinking about your answers. Be sure to respond to every statement.

Turn to the next page and begin.

Level of Loneliness Scale

	TRUE	FALSE
I feel as if nobody likes me.	1	2
I like to meet new people	2	1
I don't mind doing things alone	2	1
I have many people to talk with	2	1
I feel excluded from groups	1	2
I enjoy attending public events	2	1
I often feel sorry for myself	1	2
I never have feelings of desolation.	2	1
I feel alone a lot of the time	1	2
I have many friends	2	1
I have trouble communicating with those around me.	1	2
I will contact others without waiting for them to contact me	2	1
I feel secure in my life	2	1
I am often very anxious	1	2
I feel empty inside	1	2
I am starved for company.	1	2
I don't have anyone to depend on	1	2
I have no problem striking up conversations with strangers	2	1
I make friends easily.	2	1
I fear being rejected by others	1	2
I like most people I meet	2	1
I have nobody with whom I can share personal concerns and experiences	1	2

TOTAL = __________

Go to the Scoring Directions on the next page

Level of Loneliness Scale
Scoring Directions

The Level of Loneliness Scale is designed to help you explore the degree of your loneliness. Total the numbers that you circled on the Level of Loneliness Scale. You will get a total in the range from 22 to 44. Then, transfer this total to the space below:

LEVEL OF LONELINESS TOTAL = _________

Profile Interpretation

Individual Scale Score	Result	Indications
22 to 29	Low	Low scores indicate that you are experiencing a high level of loneliness. Complete the following exercises to develop skills for coping with the loneliness you feel.
30 to 36	Moderate	Moderate scores indicate that you are experiencing some loneliness. Complete the following exercises to develop skills for coping with any loneliness you feel.
37 to 44	High	High scores indicate that you are experiencing a low level of loneliness. Complete the following exercises to develop skills for coping with any loneliness you might feel.

Regardless of how you scored on the Level of Loneliness Scale, you will benefit from completing the activities that follow.

Situational Loneliness

Almost everyone will experience loneliness from time to time, but some people experience loneliness during a temporary situation or experience. This is usually a transient form of loneliness that changes as the situation or circumstances change.

An example of this would be moving to a new city where you do not have any friends and have not made any acquaintances. Even though this situation brings on feelings of loneliness, these feelings will gradually disappear once you have made new friends.

If you are experiencing situational loneliness, what changed in your situation?

____

____

____

What or who caused the change in your situation?

____

____

____

What is your level of loneliness?

____

       0   10

Not Very Lonely   Very Lonely

In your current situation, what can you do to be less lonely?

____

____

____

How will you know when your level of loneliness diminishes?

____

____

____

Chronic Loneliness

Chronic loneliness is a form of loneliness that persists over time, regardless of the situation or circumstances. This chronic form of loneliness usually results from a weak or non-existent support system or lack of close friends, possibly because of a personal trait such as weak social skills, shyness, or low self-confidence.

An example would be a person who lacks the self-confidence to initiate conversations when meeting new people. This type of loneliness often requires the person to take action and build a new set of social skills.

If you are you experiencing chronic loneliness, what do you think are the primary reasons?

____

____

____

Who is in your support system?

____

____

____

What is your level of loneliness?

____

       0   10

Not Very Lonely   Very Lonely

To what would you attribute the cause of your loneliness? _________________________

____

____

What can you do to overcome your loneliness? _________________________________

____

____

With whom can you discuss this? Who can brainstorm with you? ________________

____

Symptoms of Loneliness

It is important to identify the specific symptoms of loneliness you are experiencing. Because loneliness is an extreme emotional state in which people experience powerful feelings of isolation from others, it is accompanied by a variety of thoughts, behaviors and feelings.

People who are lonely will exhibit many of the following symptoms. Which do you recognize in yourself?

Place a check mark in front of the symptoms that you are able to identify.

- ❏ Feeling empty
- ❏ A sense of being hollow inside
- ❏ Crying a lot of the time
- ❏ Feeling sad
- ❏ Feeling damaged and unloved
- ❏ Feeling lost with no direction
- ❏ Feeling physical pain akin to a "broken heart"
- ❏ Feeling cutoff
- ❏ Feeling alienated from other people
- ❏ Sleep issues
- ❏ Changes in eating habits
- ❏ Feelings of depression
- ❏ Feeling as if you have no one to depend on
- ❏ Feeling self-conscious
- ❏ Convinced something is wrong with you
- ❏ Feeling disconnected
- ❏ Feeling as if you can't talk to other people
- ❏ Fearful of being in social situations

What checked item do you want to focus on first? _______________________________

What checked item do you want to focus on second? _______________________________

What checked item do you want to focus on next? _______________________________

Loneliness Sentence Starters

Loneliness can be emotionally painful.
Focus on how you feel when you are lonely?

Complete the following sentence starters to explore your feelings related to loneliness:

When I am lonely, I hurt ____

____

When I am lonely, I ache ____

____

When I am lonely, I feel sad and _______________________________________

____

When I am lonely, I feel damaged _______________________________________

____

When I am lonely, my spirit has been crushed ___________________________

____

When I am lonely, I get angry at ____

____

When I am lonely, I wish I could meet people who ________________________

____

When I am lonely, I want to be more _____________________________________

____

When I am lonely, I hate when I ____

____

When I am lonely, I envy ____

____

When I am lonely, I ____

____

What would you say is your most prominent feeling and why?

____

____

____

Like Yourself More

**Many people stay lonely because they do not like themselves enough
so they believe they need the companionship of others. In order to feel less lonely,
you need to like yourself more. Once you like yourself more, you will not feel
as sad and you will enjoy the solitude.**

In the spaces that follow, describe what you like about yourself
and what you do not like about yourself.

Things I like About Myself	How Do Others See This In Me?	How Can I Enhance This?

Things I Don't Like About Myself	How Do Others See This in Me?	How Can I Decrease This or Stop Doing This?

Expressing My Feelings

Bottling up your emotions is not healthy.
In order to overcome loneliness, you need to express your emotions.

In the spaces below, identify ways that you can express your emotions in a healthy manner.

Healthy Ways I Can Express Emotions	How I Could Begin Today	How I Could Further Engage in the Activity
Creative Activities		
Writing/Journaling		
Physical Activities		
Spiritual Activities		
Educational Activities		
Other		

In what ways do you think these activities will help you?__________________________

____

____

Escaping Loneliness

Many people who are lonely escape their feelings by engaging in unhealthy activities. What types of unhealthy activities do you engage in to avoid being lonely?

List the types of unhealthy activities you engage in, how you think they help you, and healthy activities you could engage in instead.

Unhealthy Activities	How Do You Think They Help You?	What Could You Be Doing Instead?

Which activity do you spend the most time doing, and in what ways could you begin to substitute healthier activities when you feel lonely?

____

____

____

Feeling Isolated

**The interesting thing about loneliness
is that you do not have to be alone to feel lonely.
List the situations in which there are people around, but you still feel lonely.
Describe why.**

Situations	Who is Around?	Why Do I Feel Lonely in This Situation?
1.		
2.		
3.		
4.		

What can you do in each situation to feel less lonely?

1. ____
2. ____
3. ____
4. ____

When I Am Lonely, What Am I Feeling?

It is important to focus on the feelings associated with your loneliness. Below are some of the feelings associated with being lonely.

Identify a time when you feel the loneliest, and using the feeling starters below, describe how you feel at that time.

Time when I feel the loneliest ____

Afraid____

Angry____

Apathetic ____

Ashamed ____

Bitter ____

Bored ____

Embarrassed ____

Empty ____

Envious ____

Frustrated____

Happy ____

Horrible____

Inspired____

Isolated ____

Sad ____

Scared ____

Other ____

What did you learn about yourself and your loneliness from this exercise?

____

____

____

Loneliness vs. Solitude

**It is important to distinguish between loneliness and solitude.
If you may enjoy being by yourself at times, you enjoy the solitude.
On the other hand, if there are times when you choose not to be alone,
and you find yourself feeling very isolated and alone, it may be loneliness.**

In the first table below, describe those times when you enjoy the solitude of being alone.

Times I Like to Be by Myself	What I Do During These Times	How These Activities Reassure Me

In the table below, describe those times when you do not want to be by yourself, times when you feel truly lonely.

Times I Do NOT Want to Be by Myself	What I Do During These Times	How I Feel During These Times

How can you ensure that you have more voluntary times of solitude and more time with people when you are feeling lonely?

____

____

____

Dissatisfaction with My Family and Friends

**Many people who are lonely find that they are dissatisfied
with their family and friends.**

Think about your family and friends, then describe why you feel they are not more supportive
of you. How can you elicit help to overcome your feelings of loneliness?

Family or Friend	Why I Am Dissatisfied With the Support of This Person	How This Person Could Be More Supportive

What can you say to encourage some of the people above to be more supportive?

____

____

____

My Loneliness Journal

A creative way to explore and cope with your loneliness is writing or drawing in a journal. Journaling provides an outlet to express feelings and situations you may be hesitant to discuss aloud. It can give you ideas on how to deal with problems now or in the future. An entry in your journal can be a truly cathartic experience.

By making an entry everyday about your innermost thoughts, daily struggles or major disappointments, you can work through a problem at hand and understand the way you feel about the problem.

Journaling helps reduces stress; it heals, and it helps you know and understand yourself better. Your writings may be neat or messy, paragraphs, pictures or lists, but most important is to write your feelings and observations in your journal. It will improve trust in yourself, allow you to listen to your inner voice, improve sensitivity, and allow you to write stories about your life – and share them only if you wish.

Each time you feel lonely, keep track of your feelings in your journal.
As you keep a daily log, you will begin to see patterns and common themes.

**Practice below and then continue journaling tomorrow
and each day thereafter with these same questions.**

What would it be like to not feel lonely? _______________________________

____

____

What could I do to change my attitude to be less lonely? _________________

____

____

Why am I so lonely? ____

____

____

How can I take responsibility for being less lonely? _____________________

____

____

What steps should I now take to overcome loneliness? ___________________

____

____

Visualizing Success!

People who are lonely often experience stress when thinking about upcoming social events. Visualization is a technique that can be effective in helping to reduce the stress of an upcoming social event such as a workplace party, a book club meeting or a dinner out. By practicing the technique that follows, you can reduce the stress associated with future social events.

Picture and then write about or draw a future social event that is causing you stress (bring as much detail as possible to the scene). By sharing it, you will make it real.

Imagine yourself handling the situation calmly and confidently.
Write about or draw how the successful handling of the situation will happen.

In your mind, begin to imagine yourself being successful. At the same time, rub your thumb and index finger together, or wear a piece of jewelry you can touch, and associate either one of those with the successful feeling. How does it feel?

Connected ... More? Less?

In an age in which people can connect instantly through e-mails, cell phones, Skype and other social media sites, it seems as if people would feel totally connected, but they often still feel lonely because of the lack of actual personal connection.

Think about all of the technology you use. How does it allow you to experience or prevent you from fulfilling connections with other people.

Type of Technology I Use	How I Use it to Feel Connected	How I Still Feel Disconnected

What surprises you about what you wrote?

____

____

____

____

Mother Teresa's Loneliness Quotation

> *The most terrible poverty is loneliness, and the feeling of being unloved.*
>
> **~Mother Teresa**

What is poverty? ____

____

____

____

Why do you think Mother Teresa equates loneliness with poverty? ___________________

____

____

____

In what ways do you think that loneliness is about feeling unloved? Explain. ___________

____

____

____

What does loneliness feel like to you? ________________________________

____

____

____

How does this quote relate to your life? ________________________________

____

____

My Social Circle

Your social circle is a group of socially interconnected people in your life. How can you begin to expand your social circle?

On each of the lines marked A name one person in your social circle.
On each of the lines marked B describe how or with whom you can expand your social circle?

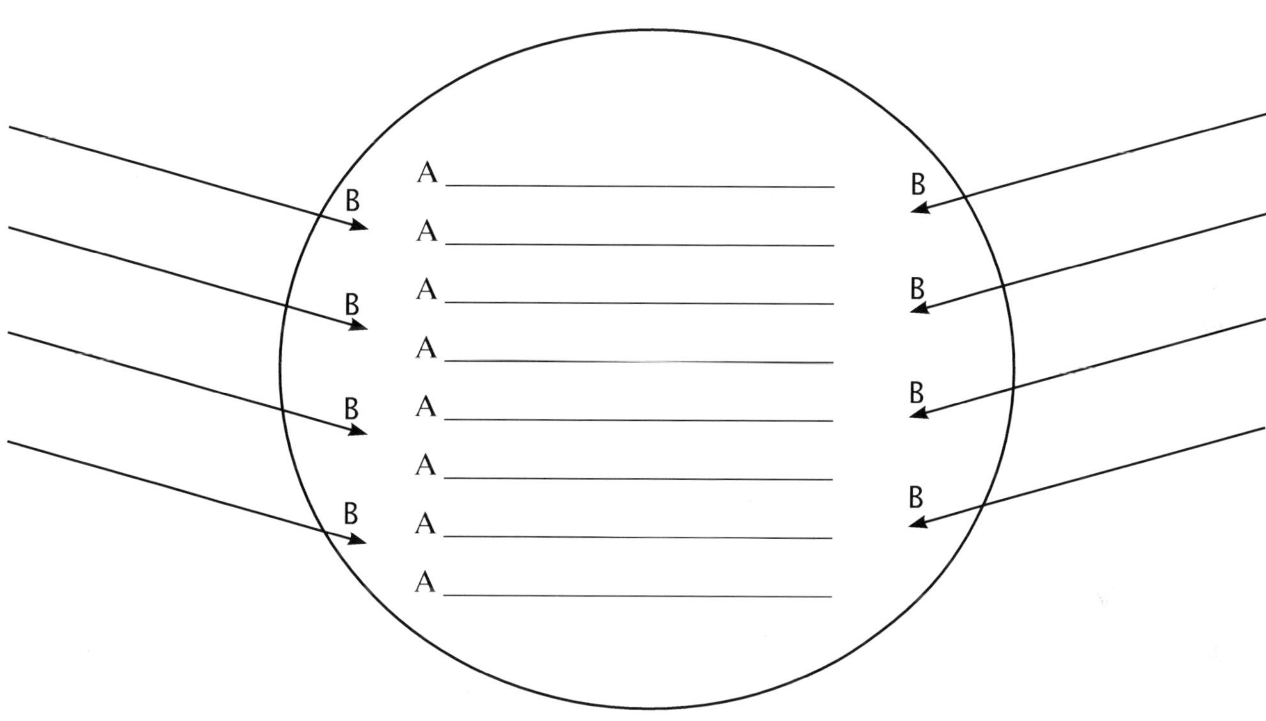

How will enriching your social circle help you to be less lonely?

____

____

____

____

Pet Companionship

Research indicates that the presence of animal companions can considerably lessen feelings of loneliness. Pets not only decrease feelings of loneliness and depression, they also can open up many opportunities for you to socialize with other pet owners (going to a pet store, dog park, people with the same type of pet or breed). Companionship that pets provide can be valuable in your ability to cope with loneliness.

Complete the table that follows:

Type of Pet	Doesn't Appeal to Me Because …	How this Type of Pet Could Benefit Me in the Future
Dog		
Cat		
Rabbit		
Guinea Pig		
Chickens		
Turtle / Tortoise		
Fish		
Other		

What has been your experience with pets in the past?

____

____

What type of pet would you consider adopting?

____

____

Personal Characteristics

Table of Contents and Facilitator Notes

Prior to distributing handouts, ask for a show of hands of those who sometimes don't want to meet new people, feel reluctant to attend social functions, or refuse to go to events.

Prior to distributing handouts, ask for examples of people they know who seem to have self-confidence, but don't. They can include themselves.

Prior to distributing handout, give a 10 to 12 second commercial about yourself.

After handouts have been completed, ask for volunteers to read their situation and the six steps on their paper.

Prior to distributing handout, ask for a show of hands of people who love to meet new people, people who are just okay with it, and those who dread meeting new people.

Prior to distributing handout, ask participants to think about some people they know. What characteristics about people turns them off?

Prior to distributing handout ask for a volunteer who would be willing to demonstrate a breathing technique in front of the others. Read the bullet points. Distribute the handout.

Prior to distributing handouts, ask for volunteers to describe aloud, in one word, what it feels like (or what thoy imagine it might feel like) to be rejected.

Prior to handouts, ask for volunteers to respond to this question: "What's the difference between being alone and being lonely?"

Table of Contents and Facilitator Notes

After participants have completed the handout, ask for volunteers to share one of their examples from the handout.

Prior to distributing the handouts, ask for a show of hands of people who are moody when they are lonely.

Prior to distributing handouts, tell group you will name several ways of communicating and ask them to put up their hands when you read the communication that they use the most. Read the following: email, a blog, social media, text, chat rooms, cell phone, land line phone, skype or face-to-face.

After handouts have been completed, ask for volunteers to share one of the scenarios described on their handout.

Prior to distributing handout, ask the group to shout out the number from 1 (being most terrifying) to 10 (being least terrifying) when they interact in large groups. Then distribute handouts.

Prior to distributing handout, ask the group: "Can anyone tell us about Maya Angelou?" You can contribute anything they've left out: Born April 4, 1928 and died May 28, 2014; she was an African-American author, poet, dancer, actress and singer.

Personal Characteristics
Introduction and Directions

People who experience loneliness often do so because of their specific personal characteristics, such as social awkwardness, introversion and/or low self-esteem. People possessing these personal characteristics are less likely to feel comfortable approaching people because they fear rejection.

This assessment contains 21 statements designed to help you explore how many of the personal characteristics that you possess are related to loneliness. Read each of the statements and decide the extent to which the statement describes you. If the statement is a lot like you, circle the 3; if the statement is somewhat like you, circle the 2; and if the statement is not like you, circle the 1.

In the following example, the circled 2 indicates the statement is **Somewhat Like** the person completing the inventory.

	A LOT LIKE ME	SOMEWHAT LIKE ME	NOT LIKE ME
I am very self-conscious	3	(2)	1

This is not a test. Since there are no right or wrong answers, do not spend too much time thinking about your answers. Be sure to respond to every statement.

Turn to the next page and begin.

Personal Characteristics Scale

	A LOT LIKE ME	SOMEWHAT LIKE ME	NOT LIKE ME

Section I

	A LOT LIKE ME	SOMEWHAT LIKE ME	NOT LIKE ME
I am very self-conscious	3	2	1
I evaluate myself negatively	3	2	1
I am preoccupied more with myself than with others	3	2	1
I don't like criticism	3	2	1
I'm afraid of embarrassing myself	3	2	1
I don't feel good about myself	3	2	1
I lack confidence in social situations	3	2	1

SECTION I Total = _________

SECTION II

	A LOT LIKE ME	SOMEWHAT LIKE ME	NOT LIKE ME
I am awkward in social situations	3	2	1
I feel uncomfortable in groups of people	3	2	1
I have trouble talking to other people.	3	2	1
I avoid social situations	3	2	1
I don't know what to say to someone I don't know.	3	2	1
I become anxious around new acquaintances	3	2	1
I don't like new and different situations	3	2	1

SECTION II Total = _________

SECTION III

	A LOT LIKE ME	SOMEWHAT LIKE ME	NOT LIKE ME
I have trouble initiating conversations	3	2	1
I am wary of intimacy.	3	2	1
I am not very assertive	3	2	1
I cannot develop relationships with strangers	3	2	1
I often feel disconnected while having conversations.	3	2	1
I am shy.	3	2	1
I have trouble connecting with others	3	2	1

SECTION III Total = _________

Go to the Scoring Directions on the next page

Personal Characteristics
Scoring Directions

The assessment you just completed is designed to measure how your own characteristics effect and/or cause your being lonely. For each of the sections on the previous page, count the scores you circled. Put that total on the line marked TOTAL at the end of each section. Then, transfer your total to the space below:

SECTION I   **Self-Esteem**   **TOTAL** _________
SECTION II   **Social Avoidance**   **TOTAL** _________
SECTION III   **Introverted**   **TOTAL** _________

To get your Grand Total, add your three scores together = _______

Profile Interpretation

Individual Section Scale Score	Grand Total	Result	Indications
7 to 11 in any single area	21 to 34 for your Grand Total	Low	Low scores indicate that certain personal characteristics of yours are not having too much effect on your loneliness. Complete the following exercises to be affected even less.
12 to 16 in any single area	35 to 49 for your Grand Total	Moderate	Moderate scores indicate that certain personal characteristics of yours are having some effect on your loneliness. Complete the following exercises to be affected even less.
17 to 21 in any single area	50 to 63 for your Grand Total	High	High scores indicate that certain personal characteristics of yours are having a great effect on your loneliness. Complete the following exercises to be affected even less.

Individual Scale Descriptions

SELF-ESTEEM – People scoring High on this scale tend not to feel good about themselves, may not be confident in social situations and worry about criticism from others.

SOCIAL AVOIDANCE – People scoring high on this scale tend to feel uncomfortable in social situations, have trouble interacting with new people and developing friendships, and avoid social situations at all costs.

INTROVERTED – People scoring high on this scale tend to be shy around other people, hesitate to ask for what they want, and have difficulty in connecting with other people.

GRAND TOTAL – People scoring high on the total of all three scales indicates that their loneliness is directly connected to low self-esteem, social avoidance, and being introverted.

My Self-Esteem

Sometimes people who are lonely are either unable or unwilling to attend social functions, or to meet new people because they have low levels of self-esteem. In order to meet new people and develop and maintain effective relationships, they need to see themselves as valuable human beings.

Complete the following chart by identifying positive accomplishments, talents, tasks that come easy to you, and character traits.

My Accomplishments (Work, family, community activities, hobbies, etc.)	**My Gifts** (Talents from all aspects of my life)
Things That Come Easy To Me (What I can do easily and well)	**My Good Character Traits** (Punctual, good listener, honest, etc.)

Developing Self-Confidence

Often, wherever we look, we see people who look very confident in themselves and their abilities. We may even think that these people were born this way. The truth is that self-confidence is something that can be developed.

Following are some of the ways you can develop your self-confidence.

Learn to smile more. Look in the mirror and smile. (A sincere smile!) How does that feel? How do you look? ______________________________________

____

____

____

Think positively. Lonely people often have many negative thoughts that keep them from reaching out to other people. What are your negative thoughts about yourself and your ability to do well in social situations? ______________________________

____

____

____

How can you turn those into positive thoughts?______________________

____

____

____

What do you really like about yourself? Why?______________________

____

____

____

Set some positive goals for yourself. Achieving them will add to your confidence. What are your goals and how can you plan to achieve them? _________________

____

____

____

My Personal Commercial

One of the best ways to develop self-confidence is to develop a personal commercial of yourself that you can say when you meet new people.

A 10-12 second commercial might go like this:

A neighbor: *I'm so sorry. I haven't introduced myself yet. I'm John.* (extend hand and shake hands) *I'm the one with the white fuzzy dog named Daisey. We walk every morning.*

Elevator: *Hi, I'm Debbie. I love your shirt. Where did you find it?*

Just moved: *Hi, My name is Ester and I just moved here. I'd love to have a cup of coffee with you to get some referrals in the neighborhood. Would you like to exchange emails?*

In general: Thank instructors, service people, anyone who helps you. You never know what comes of it!

Now you try! In the spaces that follow, develop a short commercial of yourself.

____

____

____

____

____

____

____

____

____

____

____

____

____

Once you have developed your commercial, get together with someone else in the group and take turns telling your commercial to each other.

Face Your Fears

**Loneliness is a complex emotion that can be difficult to overcome.
People experiencing loneliness often need to move out and meet people,
but are afraid to do it. In order to overcome fear, take small steps to success.**

Complete the following steps to face your fears of making social connections:

Social Situation from past____

Step 1: Ask a trusted friend to accompany you to a social event

Friend who accompanied me____

Step 2: Become familiar with the surroundings

What did your surroundings look like?______________________________________

____

____

Step 3: Notice your bodily reactions

How did your body feel?____

____

____

Step 4: Practice deep breathing or another relaxation technique

What relaxation technique did you try? _____________________________________

____

____

Step 5: Monitor your internal chatter

What negative thoughts were going through your head? ________________________

____

____

Step 6: Stay in the situation as long as possible

How did you feel the longer you stayed? ___________________________________

____

____

**Try these steps the next time you are about to face your fears, and with some
practice, you can use this strategy to feel more comfortable in a social situation!**

Making an Effort to Meet New People

Some people can meet others very easily. For some people, meeting others can be terrifying. Meeting new people does take considerable effort. One of the challenges of meeting new people is identifying places where you will feel comfortable meeting them.

Try it in the spaces below.

My Interests	Places I Could Meet People with Similar Interests	How I Could Meet them
Example: Reading	*The local bookstore*	*They have a book club that meets every Tuesday*

Which interest will you pursue in meeting new people? When and how will you proceed?

____

____

____

Driving People Away

Are you driving people away from you?
Do you have a personal characteristic that might be driving people them away?

Think about the various personal characteristics you possess that might be offensive to other people, and write about those. *(Be honest – no one else needs to see this paper!)*

My Negative Characteristic	How This Affects Others	How I Can Modify It

Social Anxiety? Panic Attacks? BREATHE

If you are like most people who become extremely anxious at the thoughts of meeting new people or being in social situations, you are looking for quick ways to reduce your anxiety. One of the first symptoms of your anxiety is your breathing becoming more shallow and quick. Learning to slow your breathing down will help to relax you and calm your anxiety.

Try the following breathing exercise. It is best if you read through the exercise and then try it.

- Sit comfortably in your chair with your back straight and your shoulders relaxed. Put one hand on your chest and the other on your stomach.

- Inhale slowly and deeply through your nose for about four seconds. The hand on your stomach should rise, while the hand on your chest should move very little.

- Hold the breath for two seconds.

- Exhale slowly through your mouth for about five seconds, pushing out as much air as you can. The hand on your stomach should move in as you exhale, but your other hand should move very little.

- Continue to breathe in through your nose and out through your mouth. Focus on keeping a slow and steady breathing pattern of 4-in, 2-hold, and 5-out.

Now answer the following questions:

How did you feel when you were trying this exercise?

____

____

____

What did you notice about your breathing?

____

____

____

In what social situations can this be beneficial for you?

____

____

____

If you feel extremely anxious and have continual panic attacks, it is probably time to see a medical professional.

Recover from Rejection

**Many people who are lonely are unwilling to take risks in reaching out
to people or taking a chance to meet new people. Rejection is a part of everyone's
life, not just yours. Be one of those people who can learn to rise above rejection
and move on with your life. Learn from your rejections.**

In the table that follows, identify times when you were rejected
and what you learned from that particular situation.

Situation in Which I Felt I was Rejected	What Happened	What I Learned
I met someone in a club.	I asked the person out on a date and was laughed at.	Not everyone will connect with me, nor I with them. It's okay.

Some affirmations about REJECTING rejection:

- **My value as a human being does not change if I am rejected.** Rejection doesn't mean anything about me, because I am the same me, regardless. No situation and no person can diminish me.

- **I can learn many things from being rejected.** I choose to trust that my life is a classroom and every experience is a perfect lesson made just for me. I can learn from each experience and be better prepared for future situations.

- **I need to evaluate** whether my feeling of rejection is actual or perceived.

- **I am as good as anyone else.** Nobody is better than me and no one is worse than me. Everyone has value. Other people are battling the fear that they aren't good enough, just like me. Everyone needs validation and encouragement.

- **I am not alone.** Many successful people in our society have the same fears as I do. They find ways to overcome their fears and success … and I can, and will, too!

Journaling about Alone Time

"There is a tremendous difference between alone and lonely.
You could be lonely in a group of people. I like being alone.
I like eating by myself. I go home at night and just watch a movie or hang out with my dog,
I have to exert myself and really say …
I've got to see my friends cause I'm too content being by myself.

~ DREW BARRYMORE

What is your level of contentment when you are by yourself?

____

____

____

Do you have a certain amount of time for being alone and then needing to be with others?
Explain.

____

____

____

What do you like to do when you're alone?

____

____

____

How do you know when you need to be with friends or family?

____

____

____

Benefit of Social Activities

When you are feeling down, your first instinct may be to hide from others and isolate yourself. This is probably one of the worst things you can do for yourself. Interacting with other people can be of tremendous help to you. When you are by yourself, you tend to sit and think too much. Thinking is a good thing, but over-thinking, especially if it's sad, negative thoughts, over and over, is not helpful.

Instead, think about some of the ways that you can continue engaging in social activities.

Social Activities	Social Activities I Enjoy	How This Helps Me
Example: Theater, Concerts, etc.	*I like going to concerts with friends.*	*We go out for dinner before or after, and have good conversation.*
Theater, concerts, etc.		
Play games		
Book clubs, classes, etc.		
Meals		
Sports-related		
Other		
Other		

What types of activities have you given up?

____

____

____

Would you consider resuming them? _____When? _______________________________

Get Involved Socially

Coping with loneliness can affect your interest in all daily activities, especially social activities. The most common reaction is to withdraw from other people and activities. When you begin to limit your social and recreational activities, you begin to physically shut down.

Think about the following sentence starters
as they relate to your participation in social and recreational activities.

One time I felt moody I ____

____

____

I (circle one) did / didn't want to be by myself because____________________________

____

____

I (circle one) did / didn't feel like being sociable so I ______________________________

____

____

I missed ____

____

____

I felt bad later because ____

____

____

I might have given others the impression that ____________________________________

____

____

I felt ____

____

____

Looking back, in the future I will ____

____

____

Techy Communications

Chatting with others, even if it is online, can help to reduce feelings of loneliness.
Respond to the sentence starters below.

The advantages of communicating with people on email are ...
____

The disadvantages of communicating with people on email are ...
____

The advantages of communicating with people on a blog are ...
____

The disadvantages of communicating with people on a blog are ...
____

The advantages of communicating with people on social media are ...
____

The disadvantages of communicating with people on social media are ...
____

The advantages of communicating with people by text are ...
____

The disadvantages of communicating with people by text are ...
____

The advantages of communicating with people on chat rooms are ...
____

The disadvantages of communicating with people on chat rooms are ...
____

The advantages of communicating with people on a cell/landline phone are ...
____

The disadvantages of communicating with people on a cell/landline phone are ...
____

The advantages of communicating with people on video calls are ...
____

The disadvantages of communicating with people on video calls are ...
____

The fun thing about communicating with people online is ...
____

The dangers of communicating with people online are ...
____

The advantages of speaking with someone face-to-face are ...
____

The disadvantages of speaking to someone face-to-face are ...
____

After responding to the sentence starters above, what have you decided are the three of the best ways for you to communicate?

1. ____

2. ____

3. ____

Reverse Your Negative Thinking

People who experience loneliness often take too much time to dwell on their negative thoughts about themselves and their lives. The good news is that it is possible to turn your negative thinking into more positive thinking.

In the table below, journal your experiences with your negative thoughts. One way to do this is to be mindful of what is happening in your own mind. In this case, mindfulness is simply attending to the stream of thoughts that go through your head when you are lonely. Look at an example:

- **Negative thoughts in my head:** "People just don't like me."
- **Feelings that follow:** Low self-esteem, emptiness, fear, hopelessness.
- **What is the evidence?** There is probably no evidence that people don't like you. Some people connect with you. You will be able to make new friends if you try. Everyone is in contact with people who connect with them and people who don't.
- **How I can reverse my thinking:** "I have had friends in the past and I will again." "I will make friends if I don't give up and if I continue engaging in social activities, where I can meet new people!"

Now that you have the formula for successfully reversing your negative thinking, try it below:

Negative Thoughts in My Head	Feelings That Follow	What is the Evidence?	How I Can Reverse My Thinking

What negative thoughts do you have about social situations?

____

____

When and where do you usually have negative thoughts? Why do you think this happened? What can you do about it?

____

____

____

Overcoming Social Anxiety

Become aware of what triggers your social anxiety and/or panic attacks look like.

Look at the following possible triggers of social anxiety.
Identify the triggers that make you the most anxious and why.
Then rank them in order, by putting a number on the line in front of each item,
from 1 (Most Terrifying) to 10 (Least Terrifying).

__________ Meet new people ____

____

__________ Be the center of attention _______________________________________

____

__________ Make small talk____

____

__________ Converse with others ____

____

__________ Speak in public ____

____

__________ Go out socially ____

____

__________ Interact in large groups ____

____

__________ Join small intimate groups ______________________________________

____

__________ Talk with important or very intelligent people_____________________

____

__________ Attend a social gathering____

____

**If you feel extremely anxious and have continual panic attacks,
it is probably time to see a medical professional.**

Maya Angelou said ...

Alone, all alone. Nobody, but nobody can make it out here alone."

~ MAYA ANGELOU

Under what circumstances can one not "make it out here alone?"

____

____

____

When is it good to be alone?

____

____

____

What's the difference between when you are alone and when you are lonely?

____

____

____

What do you think Maya Angelou was referring to when she said, "nobody can make it out here alone"?

____

____

____

Give an example of a time you experienced the thought experienced in this quotation.

____

____

____

If you are willing, share that example with others in the room.

____

____

Coping with Loneliness

After handouts are completed, ask if anyone completed the "Other" section at the bottom and if they're willing to share.

After handouts are completed, ask for volunteers to share misconceptions people might have about them, and why.

Prior to distributing handouts, ask if anyone can give the definition of dwelling (not a place to live). "Dwelling is to think, speak or write at length about a particular subject, especially one that is a source of unhappiness, anxiety or dissatisfaction."

After the handouts are completed, ask several pairs of volunteers to demonstrate the tips on the handout.

Example:

Negative Ways I Cope	Why I Do It	How It Affects Me in a Negative Way
Alcohol	I feel that I need it to get through the day	My family is upset with me, I might lose my job, I am miserable.

After handouts have been completed, ask each participant to pick one of the questions in the lower half of the page, read it, and share their response.

Prior to distributing handouts, ask for a definition of "social network." (A network of friends, colleagues, and other personal contacts.)

Table of Contents and Facilitator Notes

My Gifts	With Whom I'll Share This Gift	How I Will Share This Gift	What I Can Ask This Person to Do for Me
I love to make soup	*My 90-yr.-old neighbor*	*I can bring soup to her once a week*	*She cuts out coupons and she can give me the coupons she doesn't use that I do use.*

After handouts are completed, it might be interesting to ask the participants to share their responses to the last statement on the page.

Prior to distributing handout ask the group who likes to exercise by walking. Assuming more than one person puts a hand up, explain that this means these two or more people may have nothing else in common, but they both or all like to walk.

To Whom I Can Reach Out	How I Can Reach Out	What I Can Gain
My cousin Sue	*Make a phone call and ask if she'd like to go for a walk in the morning.*	*I don't know her well but she seems nice, likes to walk and we might become closer than we are now.*

After participants have completed the handout, ask volunteers to share their response at the bottom of the page.

Person Who Could Be a Friend	How I Know This Person	What has Stopped Me from Getting to Know the Person	What I Can Gain From Getting to Know This Person
1. Jan	*Co-worker*	*I like her but wasn't sure she'd want to be friendly with me.*	*She has many friends at work and they have lunch together.*

After handout has been completed, ask each participant to name the possibility they listed in the first column that sounds most appealing to them.

Introduce the handout by asking the group "Who is Anne Hathaway?" Ask for a volunteer to read the quotation. Discuss the fact that even young, famous, wealthy people still worry about loneliness. Then ask participants to complete the handout.

Coping with Loneliness
Introduction and Directions

Whether your loneliness is due to feeling socially awkward, personality characteristics, or a temporary change in your life, it is important that you acquire coping skills for times of loneliness. Many techniques can be used to cope with loneliness.

The *Coping with Loneliness Scale* can help you explore how well you are coping with your feelings of loneliness. This assessment contains 25 statements. Read each of the statements and decide if the statement is descriptive of you or not. In each of the statements, circle the number of your response on the line to the right of each statement.

In the following example, the circled 1 indicates that the statement is true for the person completing the scale:

	TRUE	**FALSE**
I feel like I'm the only person who is lonely	(1)	2

This is not a test and there are no right or wrong answers. Do not spend too much time thinking about your answers. Your initial response will be the most true for you. Be sure to respond to every statement.

Turn to the next page and begin.

Coping with Loneliness Scale

	TRUE	FALSE

When I am feeling the loneliest ...

		TRUE	FALSE
1.	I feel like I'm the only person who is lonely.	1	2
2.	I believe that my loneliness will never end	1	2
3.	I have negative thoughts going through my head	1	2
4.	I obsessively dwell on my past	1	2
5.	I will take risks to be with other people.	2	1
6.	I am reluctant to get involved in activities	1	2
7.	I mope about how lonely I feel	1	2
8.	I engage in my favorite hobby.	2	1
9.	I attend social functions even if I don't always feel like it	2	1
10.	I take a walk or ride a bike	2	1
11.	I go to a movie	2	1
12.	I call a friend	2	1
13.	I play with my pet or children	2	1
14.	I feel sorry for myself	1	2
15.	I wait for people to approach me	1	2
16.	I go online and surf aimlessly	1	2
17.	I try to remain positive	2	1
18.	I try to be helpful to others	2	1
19.	I turn on cheerful music	2	1
20.	I spend money on things I don't need	1	2
21.	I watch television for hours on end	1	2
22.	I use unhealthy substances	1	2
23.	I eat foods I usually don't eat.	1	2
24.	I talk with someone in my support system	2	1
25.	I attend activities in my community	2	1

TOTAL = _________

Go to the Scoring Directions on the next page

Coping with Loneliness Scale
Scoring Directions

The assessment you just completed is designed to measure how successfully you are able to cope with the loneliness in your life. For each of the items on the previous pages, count the scores you circled. Put that total on the line marked TOTAL at the end of the assessment.

Then, transfer your total to the space below:

COPING WITH LONELINESS TOTAL = __________

Profile Interpretation

Individual Scale Score	Result	Indications
25 to 33	Low	Low scores indicate that you are finding it difficult to cope with loneliness in your life. Complete the following exercises to develop greater coping skills.
34 to 41	Moderate	Moderate scores indicate that you are having some trouble coping with loneliness in your life. Complete the following exercises to develop greater coping skills.
42 to 50	High	High scores indicate that you are not having much trouble coping with loneliness in your life. Complete the following exercises to develop even greater coping skills.

Situational Loneliness

**Situational loneliness occurs when you experience temporary feelings
of loneliness due to changing life circumstances.**

In the spaces that follow, explore the circumstances in your life that have changed
or are currently changing.

A death of a loved one ...

____

____

A death of a pet ...

____

____

A break-up or divorce ...

____

____

Living without family or friends close by ...

____

____

Move to a new location ...

____

____

A mental or physical illness ...

____

____

A change of job ...

____

____

Other ...

____

____

Major Misconceptions and Fears

People who are lonely often experience many misconceptions and fears.

Complete the two sections below.

Misconceptions People Have About Me

(Example: People think I am a snob because I am not friendly in social situations.)

My Fears about Connecting with Others

(Example: I feel inadequate when I'm with people I think are smarter than I am.)

The Tendency to Dwell

**When one feels lonely, the tendency is often to obsess on why one feels that way.
To avoid dwelling on this and adding to your feelings of loneliness,
it is helpful to try different distractions.**

In the spaces that follow, draw four activities or hobbies that will help you to keep busy when you are feeling lonely. (P.S. Stick figures or magazine cutouts are okay!)

Which one will you try as soon as possible? _______________________________

Honing Your Communication Skills

In order to meet new people, or to get to know your acquaintances, try to hone your communication skills.

Some tips for being a better communicator:

- ❑ Be assertive by being open, honest and direct.
- ❑ Don't interrupt – just listen. When you interrupt you seem impatient and disrespectful to the speaker.
- ❑ Send direct, clear verbal messages.
- ❑ Pay attention to body language and gestures as well as tone, volume and pitch of voice.
- ❑ Ask for what you want and need in a respectful way.
- ❑ Be careful how many times you say, "Yes, but … ." This will begin to sound negative in your conversations.
- ❑ Focus your full attention on the speaker. Don't allow yourself to be distracted by looking at others or by looking at your watch.
- ❑ Be careful when you are communicating electronically. It is tricky to always capture exact feelings with written words.
- ❑ Know when to keep a secret and know when NOT to keep a secret if you think someone's at risk.
- ❑ Do not gossip.
- ❑ Be aware of your body language. (Eye contact, good posture, arms uncrossed, open stature, etc.)

Think of two situations coming up in which you will use your communication skills.

Situation____

____

____

Person I will communicate with _______________________________________

Conversation skills I will use ____

____

____

Situation____

____

____

Person I will communicate with _______________________________________

Conversation skills I will use ____

____

____

Negative Ways I Cope With Loneliness

**When feelings of loneliness become overwhelming,
many people will turn to negative methods to cope with their feelings.**

Complete the following table to explore your negative coping mechanisms.

Negative Ways I Cope	Why I Do It	How It Affects Me in a Negative Way
Alcohol		
Tobacco		
Drugs		
Shopping		
Eat		
Watch Television		
Self-Injury		
Sleep Issues		
Other		

I will work to develop these better strategies that I will use when I'm lonely, for example,

____

____

Responsible Conversations

Many people who find themselves experiencing loneliness have difficulty communicating effectively with others in social situations. You can learn to take responsibility for your messages and your conversations with others.

When you find yourself in a social situation, take responsibility for what you say:

Use words like I, me and my, to communicate your message. In this way you "own" the messages you send to them. Take responsibility for your own words. When you use words like "they said" or "some people," you put the responsibility of what you are saying onto someone else. Using "you" often sounds threatening, aggressive and blaming, whereas creating I-messages conveys your comments in a positive way.

Maintain eye contact and speak directly to the person. Try not to stare, look away too often, cross your arms in front of you, or allow yourself to be distracted by other sounds and sights in the environment.

Now you try! In the spaces that follow, note the questions someone might ask you, and record how you can respond.

What New People Might Ask Me	Thoughts, Ideas and Feelings I Want to Convey
Tell me a little about yourself!	
How did you decide to live here?	
How did you choose your current career path?	
What do you do with your free time?	

Now practice with someone else.

Calling all People in My Social Network

Whether you realize it or not, you have a social network. Some of the people in your social network may not live near you anymore, but they exist.

Think about your friends and family who make up your social network.
How can you establish contact with these people to get together?

Person in My Social Network and Relationship to Me	Our Communication Status	How I Can Communicate and/or Get Together with This Person More
James, my cousin	*I lost touch with him when I moved.*	*Email each other and send pictures. Maybe plan a trip to meet in the middle.*

What did you learn from this activity?

____

____

____

Ways to Share My Gifts

All people have gifts (talents) that make them unique. Being part of a community means sharing your gifts to help other people. When you do so, you connect with people in unique and different ways. (You might help a neighbor put screen doors in, while she helps you by watching your pet when you are gone for the weekend.)

Think about the gifts you have, how you could use them to help other people,
and how you can connect with other people through this barter system.

My Gifts	With Whom I'll Share This Gift	How I Will Share This Gift	What I Can Ask This Person To Do For Me

Happiness comes when we test our skills towards some meaningful purpose.

~ John Stossel

Take Risks

In order to overcome loneliness, you need to be willing to take calculated risks. These risks involve reaching out to other people and initiating a social connection.

How can you reach out to other people more effectively?

People I don't know but I would like to know, and why.

____

____

____

____

People I know a little and would like to know better, and why.

____

____

____

____

People I wish to know better than I do already, and why.

____

____

____

____

People I know, but we drifted away.

____

____

____

____

People who have experienced hardships, and ways I can help them.

____

____

____

____

Like-Minded Interests

**Like-minded interests can be a great way to enjoy yourself with others
and can be a wonderful opportunity to meet new people.
A shared interest can help you overcome your feelings of loneliness.**

Below, explore your interests and how these interests can help you meet people.

My Interests	Why I am Passionate About this Interest	How I Can Engage in this Interest with Others
Example: Exercise by walking	*Walking allows me to stay fit and see others in my neighborhood*	*The local recreation department has a walking club*

Surround yourself with only people who are going to lift you higher.

~ Oprah Winfrey

How will surrounding yourself with people who have like-minded interests "lift you higher"?

____

____

____

Friendly Invitations

**It may be time to reach out to other people
rather than sitting back and waiting for others to reach out to you.**

The table below will help you explore ways to reach out to others.

How I Can Reach Out	To Whom I Can Reach Out	What I Can Gain
Take a Walk		
Go to a Movie		
Have a Meal Together		
Do an Activity Together		
Play Cards / Games		
Other		
Other		
Other		

Your Own Company is Better Than Bad Company

Socially-well people are able to develop relationships with other people based on mutual interests. However, when you are not comfortable being by yourself, you will tend to develop relationships based on things other than mutual interests.

Identify some of the dysfunctional relationships you have developed out of neediness to be with other people. *(Examples of some dysfunctional relationships are: bullying, threats, physical, emotional, verbal and/or sexual abuse, in a relationship out of guilt, no support and/or open communication with another person, co-dependency, blamed for everything, incompatible, needs not met, feeling trapped, etc.)*

The Relationship	How the Relationship was Dysfunctional	What I Got Out of It	Was it Worthwhile?
Exmple: My neighbor	She was constantly dropping in without calling and was very needy.	It was someone to talk with and use up some of my time.	No. She was draining my energy and I needed it to stop.

Describe your plan to limit or decrease the time spent in the relationships that are not worthwhile.

____

____

____

Take Interest in People around You

**Think about likeable people you are around
but have not yet developed a relationship with them.
These people might be co-workers, neighbors, or people in your community.**

If there is a possibility of some of these likeable people becoming a friend, list them.

Person Who Could Be a Friend	How I Know This Person	What Has Stopped Me From Getting to Know the Person	What I Can Gain From Getting to Know This Person
1.			
2.			
3.			
4.			
5.			

How can you show an interest in each of these people?

1.____

2.____

3. ____

4.____

5.____

How can I ask these people about their interests?

1.____

2.____

3. ____

4.____

5.____

Get Involved

People who feel lonely can overcome their loneliness
by getting involved in activities in the community.

What types of social activities are offered in your community, local school or university, house of worship, fitness center, music groups, etc., that you might enjoy?

Possibilities	Why it Sounds Good to Me	How I Can Get More Info.
Example: Spanish class	*I studied Spanish in high school and would like to continue learning.*	*I will talk with admissions reps from my local community college.*

Which two of the above sound most appealing? _______________________________________

____

When will you start investigating? ____

____

My Least Favorite Thing

> *"Loneliness is my least favorite thing about life.
> The thing that I'm most worried about is just being alone
> without anybody to care for or someone who will care for me."*
>
> **~Anne Hathaway**

Read the Anne Hathaway quote above and then answer the following questions:

Do you worry about being alone without anyone to care for? Explain.

____

____

____

____

____

Do you worry about being alone without anyone to care for you? Explain.

____

____

____

____

How can you build your own support network, to ensure always having people to rely on?

____

____

____

____

____

Alone Time

Prior to distributing handouts, ask if anyone can tell the group anything about Henry David Thoreau. Thoreau (1817–1862) was an American author, poet, philosopher, polymath, abolitionist, naturalist, tax resister, development critic, surveyor, historian, and leading transcendentalist. He is best known for his book "Walden," a reflection upon simple living in natural surroundings. Read the quotation aloud and then distribute handouts.

Example:
When I am alone, I can finish the following projects______ (I started to journal every night.)
When I am alone, I cannot finish the following project____ (Balancing my checkbook because I can't concentrate or focus.

After handouts are completed, ask for volunteers to share their responses to the last question on the page.

Prior to distributing handout, ask the group for a show of hands if they agree that all people should spend some time alone every day. Distribute handouts.

After handouts are completed, brainstorm the various results of the handout.

After handouts are completed, brainstorm the various results of the handout.

After handouts are completed, ask participants to share items they wrote in the "Other" rows. They might include playing solitaire, bowling, taking a ride, travel, etc.

After participants complete the page, ask two volunteers, one who wants constant contact with their partner, and one who needs alone time, to role play a conversation without their scripts, telling each other how they feel.

Table of Contents and Facilitator Notes

After handouts are completed, ask participants to share the activities they will consider.

After handouts are completed, ask participants how they can make new friends or connect with old ones.

Prior to distributing handouts, ask for a show of hands. How many people have a cell phone, land line, computer, equipment that has games, etc.

After handouts have been completed, ask participants to share their response to this item: "Volunteer to help others. How can you do this?"

After handouts are completed, ask for volunteers to share something they wrote in the "Other" row. Possible examples: I come off as stuck-up even though I am just shy – or - I have unfriendly body language.

Prior to distributing handouts, ask "What are core beliefs?"
Core beliefs are the very essence of how we see ourselves, other people, the world, and the future.

After handouts are completed, go around the room and ask participants to read their responses to the last question on the page.

After handouts are completed, ask participants to read their responses to the last question on the page.

After distributing the handouts, ask for four volunteers, each to read one of the quotations aloud. Participants can either complete the handout alone or form into four groups, everyone choosing the quotation they want to discuss, get together in a corner of the room, discuss their quotation and write their various thoughts. Afterwards, they can share them with everyone.

Alone Time
Introduction and Directions

Loneliness is a feeling that people experience when they feel disconnected from people who are no longer there. This disconnect can be related to such occurrences as a relationship break-up, divorce, death, separation, or moving to a different city. When you are lonely you feel bad.

On the other hand, **alone time** is simply enjoying, or not enjoying being with yourself. It is a state of mind in which you either cherish being alone, or you don't like it. When you are alone, you can find that there are many positive ways to enjoy alone time. Once you enjoy being alone you will be more content and peaceful, and become your own person, not defined by anyone else.

The *Alone Time Scale* will help you explore whether or not you enjoy being alone.

This assessment contains 24 statements related to being alone. Read each of the statements and decide whether or not the statement describes you. If the statement *does* describe you, circle the number in the YES column. If the statement *does not* describe you, circle the number in the NO column. Do not pay attention to the numbers following the statements.

In the following example, the circled number under YES indicates the statement is descriptive of the person completing the scale.

	YES	**NO**
I do not enjoy spending time by myself	(1)	2

This is not a test and there are no right or wrong answers. Do not spend too much time thinking about your answers. Your initial response will be the most true for you.
Be sure to respond to every statement.

Turn to the next page and begin.

Alone Time Scale

	YES	NO
I do not enjoy spending time by myself	1	2
It is liberating to spend time alone	2	1
Being by myself can be enriching	2	1
I tend to feel sad when I am alone	1	2
I'm comfortable in my own company	2	1
I cherish my alone time	2	1
Some of my most creative moments occur when I'm by myself	2	1
I think about too many sad things when I am alone	1	2
I enjoy not having to rely on anyone but myself	2	1
I become very negative when I am alone	1	2
I am content doing activities by myself	2	1
I don't like being with myself	1	2
I like being with people and I like my alone time	2	1
I enjoy peaceful solitude	2	1
I feel cut off from others when I'm alone	1	2
I like to be able to do something when I feel like doing it	2	1
I feel secluded when I'm alone	1	2
I don't like eating a meal alone	1	2
I can work, think or rest when I'm alone	2	1
I see things more clearly when I have alone time	2	1
I choose to be all alone at times	2	1
When I'm alone, I tend to feel sorry for myself	1	2
I crave human interaction at all times	1	2
When I have alone time, I get my life together	2	1

TOTAL = _________

Go to the Scoring Directions on the next page

Alone Time Scale
Scoring Directions

There is a big difference between begin alone and being lonely. Being alone can be a positive and rewarding experience for some people, and for others, it is not. Being lonely is always a negative experience. It is critical to be aware of those times when you are simply alone, versus the times when you are feeling lonely.

The *Alone Time Scale* is designed to help you explore whether or not you enjoy being alone. On the previous page, add the numbers that you circled and write the score on the TOTAL line.

You will receive a total in the range from 24 to 48. Then, transfer that number to the space below.

Alone Time Total = __________

Profile Interpretation

Scale Score	Result	Indications
24 to 31	low	You are experiencing many negative feelings related to being alone. You have a tremendous need to be with and connect with other people. You are not content with alone time.
32 to 40	moderate	You are experiencing some negative feelings related to being alone. You like to be with and connect with other people. You are somewhat content with your alone time.
41 to 48	high	You are experiencing few negative feelings related to being alone. You have sufficient social connection with other people. You are content with your alone time.

Scale Descriptions

Alone Time — People scoring high on this scale tend to feel okay being by themselves. Alone can be a positive state of mind in which you feel happy by yourself. You do not need to be with others to feel content. You find that being by yourself can be an uplifting and peaceful experience. People scoring low do not enjoy their alone time.

No matter how you scored on the Alone Time Scale (Low, Moderate or High), you will benefit from doing all of the following exercises. These activities are for people who enjoy being alone and also for those who do not.

"I Love to be Alone..." Quotation

"I love to be alone. I never found the companion
that was so companionable as solitude."

~ Henry David Thoreau

Think about the quote you just read.
Answer the following questions in the spaces below:

What do you think about this quote?

____

____

____

____

____

____

____

How does or doesn't it apply to your life?

____

____

____

____

____

____

____

____

Can or Can Not?

**Some people choose to be alone! They are able to enjoy time by themselves.
Others do not!
Whether you do or do not, think about all of the positive things you are able,
or would be able to do when you are alone.**

Complete the following sentence starters:

When I am alone, I can finish the following projects______________________________

____

When I am alone, I cannot finish the following projects__________________________

________________________________because__________________________________

____

When I am alone, I can accomplish ____

____

When I am alone, I cannot accomplish______________________________________

________________________________because__________________________________

When I am alone, I love being able to______________________________________

____

When I am alone, I am not able to ____

________________________________because__________________________________

____

When I am alone, I have time to ____

____

When I am alone, I have time to ____

________________________________but I don't because ______________________

When I am alone, I am creative with ______________________________________

____

When I am alone, I am unable to be creative with __________________________

________________________________because__________________________________

____

When I am alone, I feel like ____

____

____

____

A Benefit ... or Not?

Being alone can be a positive experience and a welcome change, or not.

Following are some of the ways that people can benefit from being alone, or not.

Relaxation – Are you able to relax when you are alone? Why or why not?

____

____

____

____

Thinking Time – Does contemplation during alone time benefit you or not? Explain.

____

____

____

____

Spending Time with Others – Does this work for you or not? Explain.

____

____

____

____

Independence – Does being alone help you to be more self-reliant, or not? Explain.

____

____

____

____

Do you have any other thoughts about being alone?

____

____

____

____

Spend Time ALone

Tenzin Gyatso, the 14th Dalai Lama, suggested that all people

"Spend some time alone every day."

When is the best time each day that you could spend quality time alone?
How would you use this time alone?

When Can You Spend Time Alone Each Day?	What Will You Do During This Time?	How Will This Help Your Overall Well-Being?

How can this alone time allow you to feel more comfortable?

____

____

____

My Alone-Time Positive Feelings

**It's important to explore the wide range of positive feelings
you may be experiencing when you are alone.**

In the following spaces, using the following scale, rate the extent of your positive feelings
when you are by yourself, and describe what it feels like in the space that follows.

Not Positive at All		**Somewhat Positive**		**Extremely Positive**
0	3	5	7	10

Content = ________

____

Self-Sufficient = ________

____

Creative = ________

____

Calm = ________

____

Connected to the Universe = ________

____

Spiritual = ________

____

Hopeful = ________

____

My Alone-Time Negative Feelings

**It's important to explore the wide range of negative feelings
you may be experiencing when you are alone.**

In the following spaces, using the following scale, rate the extent of your negative feelings
when you are by yourself, and describe what it feels like in the space that follows.

Not Positive at All		**Somewhat Positive**		**Extremely Positive**
0	3	5	7	10

Cut off from the world = _________

____

Alienated = _________

____

Anxious = _________

____

Hopeless = _________

____

Unimaginative = _________

____

Unloved = _________

____

Depressed = _________

____

Ways to Be More Content

You might enjoy your alone time more, or begin to enjoy your alone time, if you identify some ways to spend your time.

In the spaces that follow, explore the various ways you might enjoy your alone time.

Ways to Spend My Time	How I Can Do This	How It Will Help Me
Start a new hobby		
Exercise more		
Limit television/computer		
Sing, dance, journal		
Enjoy a pet		
Help someone in need		
Go to movies, theater, concerts, museums		
Walk outdoors		
Volunteer		
Other		

Which of these options will you begin to implement immediately and how?

____

____

UH OH! We Have a Problem!

**Often, two people living in the same home have differing views on alone time.
Person #1 values, needs and wants some alone time.
Person #2 does not value, need or want alone time and wants to be together 24/7.**

Create a conversation between the two, explaining how they each feel about their alone time.

#1 ____

____

#2 ____

____

#1 ____

____

#2 ____

____

#1 ____

____

#2 ____

____

Create a conversation between the two, coming up with a compromised solution.

#1 ____

____

#2 ____

____

#1 ____

____

#2 ____

____

#1 ____

____

#2 ____

____

With your script, role-play with someone else in the room, who will represent the opposite issue as yours.

(Continued on the next page)

UH OH! We Have a Problem! *(Continued)*

Since alone time means different things to different people, it can be very difficult when you live with another person who has different ideas about the value of alone time.

In the spaces that follow, describe your current situation (or a situation from the past in which this was the case) and how you can develop a plan so that both of you can enjoy your time together and your alone time.

Person #1 values, needs and wants some alone time. Who is this (you or a partner, spouse, roommate, etc.)? ____

Describe your or the other person's need for alone time. _______________________________

____

Person #2 does not value, need or want alone time and wants to be together 24/7.
Who is this (you or a partner, spouse, roommate, etc.)?_________________________________

____

What are ways that both person #1 and person #2 can be satisfied?

____

____

____

How could you (and the other person) accomplish this?

____

____

____

What would each of you have to sacrifice?

____

____

____

If you succeeded in working this out, how would it affect your relationship?

____

____

____

What To Do?

Whether you enjoy being alone or not:

- Circle items you enjoy doing by yourself or doing with others you do not know.
- Check items you are willing to try.
- Put a line through the items you would not consider.

❏ Antique shop	❏ Hike	❏ Silversmith
❏ Artwork	❏ House of worship	❏ Sing
❏ Astronomy class	❏ Investment club	❏ Social media
❏ Auction	❏ Jigsaw puzzle	❏ Solitaire
❏ Bicycle ride	❏ Lapidary	❏ Sports
❏ Billiard	❏ Learn a language	❏ Stained glass
❏ Bird watch	❏ Library	❏ Store sales
❏ Blog	❏ Mah Jongg	❏ Swimming
❏ Book club	❏ Martial arts	❏ Theater
❏ Bowling league	❏ Models	❏ Thrift store
❏ Card club	❏ Movies	❏ Travel
❏ Ceramics	❏ Museums	❏ Volunteer
❏ City club/rotary	❏ Musical instrument	❏ Walk outside
❏ College course	❏ Natural Health	❏ Water aerobics
❏ Computer	❏ Online scrabble	❏ Woodworking
❏ Cooking class	❏ Photography	❏ Writing
❏ Crafts	❏ Piano lessons	❏ Yoga
❏ Crossword puzzle	❏ Poetry	❏ Zoo
❏ Cruise	❏ Political club	❏ Other
❏ Dance	❏ Pool	❏ Other
❏ Drumming	❏ Quilting	❏ Other
❏ Exercising	❏ Read	❏ Other
❏ Genealogy	❏ Restaurant	❏ Other
❏ Go to the gym	❏ Sewing	❏ Other

Share with others why you enjoy doing the items you circled and why you would consider the items that you checked.

Expanding Your Alone Time

**To be in healthy relationships with other people,
it is helpful to experience the joy of being alone.
Spend several hours by yourself, and then reflect on the following questions.**

What did you learn about yourself from being alone?

____

____

____

What negative feelings did you experience?

____

____

____

What positive feelings did you experience?

____

____

____

How did you spend this alone time? Was it productive?

____

____

____

What happened that you did not expect to happen?

____

____

____

Now that you have spent a little time by yourself, try expanding this alone time until you are satisfied and content in your own company. If that doesn't work, it's time to make new friends or connect with old friends.

How Much Tech is Too Much Tech?

**Some people use social media, cell phones, etc., during their alone time.
This can serve to be distracting but if too much time is spent, it can also limit the
time you spend doing other things more useful or creative and/or limit your time
interacting with other people in person.**

Think about how much time you devote to social media relationships
and what you receive from them by answering the questions below:

Approximately how much time per day do you spend interacting with people on social media sites, or the computer, etc., time in general?

Chat rooms. . . . . = _______	Texting. . . . . = _______
Online dating sites . . . . = _______	Searching . . . . = _______
Online groups. . . . . = _______	Other_________________ = _______
Emailing . . . . = _______	Other_________________ = _______
Video chatting . . . . = _______	Other_________________ = _______
Games . . . . = _______	Other_________________ = _______

How does this form of connection help you with your alone time?

____

____

How does it keep you from spending time with other activities or people?

____

____

How can you make a pledge to yourself to cut down on some of time spent on the above list and use that time in other beneficial ways?

____

____

Are you always honest about who you are when you are online? _______________________

Do you believe other people are always honest with you online? _______________________

If there is dishonesty, what does that say about an online relationship?

____

____

Developing Friendships

There are actually many things you can do to develop healthy relationships and ensure that you are not experiencing feelings of loneliness.

Following are some tips, and questions you can answer,
to help you develop friendships with others.

Take better care of your personal appearance and hygiene. How can you do this?

____

____

____

Show people that you are interested in what they are saying. How can you do this?

____

____

____

Ask people questions that show you are interested in them. How can you do this?

____

____

____

Get involved in community activities. How can you do this?

____

____

____

Volunteer to help others. How can you do this?

____

____

____

(Continued on the next page)

Developing Friendships *(Continued)*

Call or visit friends and family. How can you do this?

____

____

____

____

Adopt a pet for companionship. How can you do this?

____

____

____

____

Go places to be around other people. How can you do this?

____

____

____

____

Believe that others will like you. How can you do this?

____

____

____

____

Don't be disappointed if you don't connect. How can you do this?

____

____

____

____

"Pushing" Others Away

**One reason you may not be connecting with others
is that you may be unconsciously pushing people away from you.**

Think about situations in which you did not feel welcome around others.
How might you be pushing people away from you?

Ways I May Be Pushing People Away	How I Might Be Doing This	How I Can Do Better
I often focus on the negative		
I do not always listening attentively		
I do not always consider the other's needs		
I sometimes ask too many personal questions		
I often talk only about myself		
I am argumentative		
I saying hurtful things without meaning to		
Other		

Unrealistic Core Beliefs

**People who would prefer not being alone might feel very lonely.
They often have an unrealistic set of core beliefs that limit them
from reaching out to other people and developing healthy social connections.**

In the spaces that follow, examine your core limiting beliefs by placing an X in front of the beliefsyou have about yourself, and try to identify the evidence (if there is any) to support these beliefs:

I feel that ...

______Nobody loves me. ____

____

______I am unsure of myself. ____

____

______I am not fun to be around. _______________________________________

____

______I have a dull personality. ____

____

______I make others nervous. ____

____

______I can't talk to people I don't know. ______________________________

____

______Nobody cares about what I have to say. ___________________________

____

Now think about how unrealistic and irrational some of these thoughts are. If you were very honest, you possibly had a difficult time finding evidence for many of your negative core beliefs. If you did find evidence for a negative core belief, try changing it with positive affirmations.

For example, you could say: "I am fun to be around."

"When I am with people who have similar interests as I do,
I am outgoing."

"I have a great personality!"

"I am a very nice person!"

NOW YOU TRY!

Connecting with People Like Me

If you prefer not having a lot of alone time, it may be time to develop or enhance relationships. It is important to develop relationships with people who are like you, with similar attitudes, interests and values.

In the table below, identify the people in your life, and ways they are like you, and how you could connect better with them.

Name of Person in My Life	Attitude	Interests	Values	How I Could Connect With This Person

Where can you go to find new people who have attitudes, interests and values similar to yours?

____

____

____

Make an Effort

**To be alone less, it's probably time to step up your friendships.
This will take energy and courage on your part, but it will be beneficial.
Think about the people you could ask to share a fun activity.**

Complete the table that follows.

People I Could Ask	An Activity We Could Share	Why This Person?
Example: *Sherry*	*Go to a movie*	*Sherry has always been a friend, but we are both shy. She loves movies.*

Who is the first person you will contact? Why?

____

____

____

Quotations – Can You Relate?

Write your thoughts under each of the four quotations below.

*"Let me tell you this: if you meet a loner, no matter what they tell you,
it's not because they enjoy solitude. It's because they have tried
to blend into the world before, and people continue to disappoint them."*
~ Jodi Picoult

---

*"I care for myself. The more solitary, the more friendless, the more unsustained I am,
the more I will respect myself."*
~ Charlotte Brontë

"If you're lonely when you're alone, you're in bad company."
~ Jean-Paul Sartre

"It is far better to be alone that to wish you were."
~ Ann Landers

Now, create your own quotation about aloneness, as it relates to you.

Whole Person Associates is the leading publisher of training resources for professionals who empower people to create and maintain healthy lifestyles. Our creative resources will help you work effectively with your clients in the areas of stress management, wellness promotion, mental health and life skills.

Please visit us at our web site: **Wholeperson.com**. You can check out our entire line of products, place an order, request our print catalog, and sign up for our monthly special notifications.

Whole Person Associates

800-247-6789